More Empathic Indulgence

Love, loss, and inspiration in life

Jeremy Mckemy

BookLeaf Publishing

India | USA | UK

Made with ❤ on the BookLeaf Publishing Platform
www.bookleafpub.in
www.bookleafpub.com

Dedication

To my Mom,

You've been nothing short of a super hero in my life, you are always there when I fall to pick me back up, cheer me up when I'm sad, calm me when I'm mad, the voice of reason, forever my hero!! You're an inspiration!! Salt of the earth. My biggest supporter in this life, you mean the world to me. My true OG best friend. You will always be my absolute rock! I absolutely love and adore you!! This book is dedicated to you!!

Preface

This book has been a culmination of the past year's losses and triumphs. From my insecurities to my eagerness to find myself. Mixed emotions and self loathing, to elated feelings of joy and childhood memories. A real rollercoaster.

Acknowledgements

I want to acknowledge all my friends who put up with my antics as I wrote the poems included in this book and the last year of my writings. I know it can get overwhelming reading them and it's sometimes daunting and erratic. So thank you to my special Doctor, thank you to my cousin Denny, and all the rest of my friends and family. Thank you to my rescue Buddy!! I think he rescued me that day at the humane society. That unconditional love and bond is strong as an oak.

1. 1000 MPH

My heart is Lost in this world,
And it's Spiraling at 1000 miles and hour,
It's On a collision course,
But I'm Standing too tall to cower,
My heart is Leaking my sanity,
Gripping me with all its power,
Poised through process,
Like a withering flower,
So pretty,
For only a moment since,
So pretty,
Past present future tense,
It's Chaos in control,
With Me safe inside my imaginary fence,
As the universe loses me,
In its cynical defense,
Always yearning to break free,
But lost when I do,
All these uncontrollable feelings,
Feelings From black to blue,

What's true is true,
From what ensues,
But it keeps pumping,
Beat after beat,
Every single time,
Never to admit defeat.

2. 5 am

5 am
2 whiskeys in,
Putting in the work,
All the feelings felt,
All the responsibility's to shirk,
Depression is a lonely thing,
When your cringing on the inside,
Your singer won't sing,
Your ringer won't ring,
You just wish the worst,
When we are feeling like this,
A feeling like your gonna burst,
Or explode which is worse,
You don't wanna anybody to catch the flack,
The flack of your heart exploding that you can't get back,
You can't,
Doesn't work like that,
Then it's over then its splat,
Your a bug on loves windshield,
Squashed heart all shattered,

Washing away the mess,
Making a mess of me,
Smeared and splattered,
Washed with the rains of time,
Might take a while,
And sometimes your outa spray,
The tears that wash it all away,
Your left with aguish,
Hurting inside,
Invisible scars,
Cut deep and too the bone,
Too many scars,
I don't wanna face this world alone,
I know god has my back,
Bring me back from despair,
Bring me back to reality,
Please don't make me,
Just another one of loves fatality's!

3. 100% connected

How lonely is a free bird,
Wandering without want or need,
With all his demons,
Picking at the seemingly free bird seed,
Twisted inside are all the thoughts,
Ever so intrusive and mean,
Such a impairment to carry,
Burden of the weight,
Twisting and writhing,
Searching for the gate,
Knowing where you belong,
Though your afraid your late,
But they are playing your song,
Intrigued by the way shit tumbles,
Falls into place,
When you take the chance,
And Play with the ace,
You don't just finish the battle,
You exceed expectations,
And take your place

Upon the pinnacle of the mountain,
Way above the face,
All along trying not to wig out,
End up a lonely man,
Certified basket case.

4. Cosmic bliss

Rest easy and smile,
Just beam with pride,
Your special kind,
Filled with love and laughter,
Passion Divine,
Like a gift from heaven,
Sacramental wine,
Selfless like a saint,
So much gusto,
You brush it on like paint,
God moved the sky,
And placed it in your eyes,
I gaze upon them with wonder,
With you,
I can really fly,
Feet have left the ground,
Floating off into the sky,
Wanting to be on your ride,
Set all that aside,

I've never felt like this,
And that's no lie.

5. Super Blue

It's been a year,
Since my feelers were opened,
Since the greatest night of my life,
Feeling love for the first time,
For More than a decade it eluded me,
Super blue moon love reared its head,
Now it included me,
I can feel again,
Write what's going on my head,
Put pen to paper,
I thought I was dead,
Rotten inside,
All the love was lost,
To far gone,
It was just in a corner,
Ready to sing that song,
It came out that super blue moon,
When our lips touched,
And the girl of my dreams wanted me,
I never thought it would happen,

I wasn't ready,
When you straddled me,
Opened Pandora's box,
A love so big,
It can now never be lost,
I guess we weren't ready,
I blew my chance somehow,
I guess I was unsteady,
But know my love it true,
And extremely heavy,
I found a bright soul in you,
Oh how we align,
We belong together,
Like a fantastic design,
Peas and carrots,
Just know I'm inclined,
To keep our friendship alive,
Friendship refined,
Our souls intertwined,
Two amazing people,
Then let the Good times combine,
Then you have a year of love,
A year of friendship redefined.

6. Happy Buddy

I can't explain,
The happiness I'm feeling,
Now I have my Buddy,
My serotonin is reeling,
My new best friend,
How my love is bubbling,
Feeling this feeling again is amazing,
No worries,
Nothing troubling,
Feeling euphoric,
Down right giddy,
Like the first time,
I ever experienced a city,
The feel good,
Feels so good,
So much affection,
Like he's been in my embrace forever,
Love and self reflection,
This love won't fade,
Never,

It'll only grow,
Wider and deeper,
Day by day,
With this amazing creature,
He follows me from room to room,
Follow the leader,
I got a lot to learn about love,
Dogs as my teacher,
Unconditional love,
Loves ultimate feature,
Natures natural,
Heart feelings weaver,
Warm and fuzzy,
Life long procedure!

7. Thoughts outa control

7

Soaking away,
Bobbing in this tub,
Wondering how,
I'm Suppose to care,
When I'm just bobbing here,
Without a care,
Do I dare,
Keep up the journey,
No time to spare,
In my glass house,
Stones are being thrown,
It's infested with doubt,
There goes a mouse,
I'll sit here and pout,
Coughing and sputtering,
Wanting to shout,
But I calmly contemplate,
What's next,

Am I really a good person,
Or am I simply dead weight,
Swirling thoughts rattle around my brain,
Am I actually a benefit to this world,
Or a mere stain,
Bloodying a white shirt,
You can't erase it,
Boy does it hurt,
Bleeding out all the passion,
Pumping life blood with every squirt,
All I can do is aspire to be better,
Keep up the positive stuff,
Quit complaining of the weather,
Stuff outa my control,
I'm ripping up this life,
Yes I'm the bull,
Taurus all the way,
The China shop is fucked,
Hoping to bring back happiness,
Trying not to deconstruct,
Bring fourth joy,
With all the love I can conduct!!

8. Torture

When you are fallen,
Slipped through the cracks,
Too many times you rose up,
Now your flat on your back,
Just know life keeps going,
Putting you through the ringer,
Your a busy bee,
Don't remove your stinger,
Take the torture,
Don't give in to the pain,
Know you can take it,
The Deep dark destain,
The endless mindfulness,
Awake in misfortune,
Aware,
Taking tortures portion

9. Tourniquet

Damage is done,
Heart strained,
Too much,
Non temporary pain,
Will I ever heal,
Be still my heart,
Less the destain,
Bringing the waterworks,
Not talking the rain,
Not a option,
To refrain,
Keep looking forward,
Frame by frame,
Step by step,
Heartache outa my heart,
Quiet my brain,
Quit the hurt,
Stop the bleeding,
It will be worth it,
Please God,

Patch me up,
The perfect Dr,
The way only you can lord,
High on the cross,
Fix my heart,
It's a sure fit,
I beg of you lord,
Put on a tourniquet!

10. Mulligan

New beginnings,
Started healing,
New feeling,

Finally slept,
Heart unkept,
Soul swept,

Fresh dealings,
Higher ceilings,
So so appealing,

Where to start,
From a broken heart,
Gotta be smart,

Take it easy,
Just need a gal to please me,
Easy peasy lemon squeezy.

11. Double on the rocks

Sipping life like whiskey on the rocks,
Truth be told,
I'm stuck in the boondocks,
Pickup trucks,
And the long walk to the mailbox,
Childhood memories of lost country roads,
Outdoors with gardens and animals,
A-team and dukes of hazard episodes,
Swimming pools with filter checks,
Chlorine tablets and toads,
My child hood remembered all these fond nights,
Cousins a many,
And first feeding rights,
Chicken coops grabbing fresh eggs,
Riding bikes till your shaking,
Wore out legs,
Swimming till dark and then it's game time,
Aggravation and the coolers of wine,
I'm talking boons farm,
Gawking at the pines,

Shooting all day with no thought till tomorrow,
Wondering if it would ever end,
Then comes tomorrow,
As she summers ended and things returned to normal,
Then came school and all the things that were formal,
Just know our childhood was anything other normal,
It was all exceptional,
Way out of the ordinary,
It was quite the best,
Nothing short of Extraordinary!!

12. Withered

Withered is the sense of elated feelings,
In there place is that of regret,
Did I squander the last years,
Lost in lonely I regress,
Too many empty nights,
Playing with my empty soul,
Put out for all to see,
How can I love another,
When myself is the one I need,
Self love is far from my grasp,
Yearning to gain it,
As it eludes my reach,
Just knowing I'm human,
When life lesson is all that I teach,
Do what I say,
Not what I do,
I have great advice,
Just don't walk in my shoes,
It's not all rainbows and glitter,

Being this crazy without self love,
Lost and insecure,
You found me,
Sprawled out on the floor,
All covered in bad memories,
With self loathing to explore,
So pour me another whiskey,
And bring me another song,
I'll love my life,
I'll stay strong,
I'll live it the way I know how,
With all my heart,
Holier than thou,
Horse before the cart,
With the good lord on my side,
Guiding me on my personal plight,
Living in the now,
Knowing I'm right,
When I can't let go of the past,
It brings me to tears,
Because I'm so much better,
Than all the lost years,
I need to catch up fast,
I'm in the new man,
I've Left the old to die,
I'll be here living,
With a great life to try,

Bringing my best foot in the front,
When all I want is joy,
But Some times you have to punt,
To get ahead of the opponent,
Grit your teeth and grunt,
But I'll find that love,
Life's little stunt,
I'm on my way up,
This dog will hunt,
It's Floating around in my heart,
It's so prevalent,
It's just gotta get warmed up,
Then it'll fire up and start,
Self love is incoming,
Never to part,
Never to make me wonder,
If I'm good enough,
Or am I bad,
Demons to drag me under,
When the good in me picks me up,
Good times are ahead,
With Many future memories to plunder,
I'll always wonder,
Am I good,
Or is it good that I hunger,
I try to bring wholesome vibes,
With all my actions,

Make people happy,
Barring all infractions,
Knowing I don't always succeed,
Max impaction,
But I'll keep trying to make a good impact,
Bring fourth glad tidings and good intentions,
And keeping my sanity,
With free will and life's emotional inventions,
All the while,
Living life's intervention.

13. One

When will I find a heart,
One that loves like mine,
One that can see past my faults,
One that want to dance my dance,
One that wants me and her to waltz,
One that want to hold me,
One that wants to know me,
One that brings me complete happiness,
One that brings that scrappiness,
One that wants to connect,
One that I can respect,
One that does what needed to be fair,
One that doesn't mind my stare,
One that likes my weird quirky ways,
One that doesn't tire of my boring days,
One that can love hard and deep,
One that can love like a Shepard loves his sheep,
One that's kind and generous with there love,
I ask this of the universe,
From the one and only God up above!!

14. New to me

I'm ready for a new me,
Self care,
Positive like a honey bee,
Deep,
Lasting changes like a redwood tree,
I'm a tiger,
I'm changing my stripes,
Good things,
Less and less gripes,
Live in the now,
No more chasing snipes,
Live in today,
Love flowing like a waterfall,
Self love,
Higher self worth will be the protocol,
Integrity,
Joy in life is my Tylenol,
In the present,
No more mental block,
Sidestep,

Knowing I can be a rock,
Full of wisdom,
Ready to walk the walk,
Truth,
Not just talk the talk,
Time eternal ,
Life on my own clock,
Happy,
Don't let others darken my brilliancy,
My Shine,
Keep up my amazing resiliency,
Overcome,
Show my adaptability,
Live life,
With intense integrity,
Lose all,
Each and every negativity,
Give it all,
Live with never ending bravery

15. Golden years

When the inevitable kicks in,
Life that has been going since I born,
I wanna stay forever also,
But my body is so worn,
Giving up it's Warrenty,
We were never promised,
No known guarantee,
Just averages,
What is the norm,
Will you make it too your golden years,
Physically unharmed or ripped and torn,
Everybody is different,
Plight of decent man,
Trying pass this stage,
Me being a flash in a pan,
My existence is positive,
My heart is warm and passionate,
My heart is stitched to my sleeve,
Where life has fastened it.

I have much to give,
Spreading all that love,
Till I've mastered it.

16. Wasted

Wasted times and wasted chances,
Too many false starts,
Not enough first dances,
So many broken hearts,
Another drink and some more advances,

Just know I ain't done asking,
Throwing myself out there,
Dragging this net I'm casting,
Drinking this beer,
Getting these hangovers I'm amassing,

Mutual attraction is needed,
A soft touch from me,
Two way affection I'm pleading,
For both of our sakes,
Otherwise our hearts are defeated,

Just knowing we are on the same page,
Reading the same book,

Not different places or in a different cage,
Too much one way effort,
Put ones heart in a rage,

Then it's bound to come out,
In sloppy form,
With a heartfelt rant and shout,
A horrible hangover
Then days of tears and a lot of doubt,

I guess sometimes its just not right,
The fit is wrong,
Without a disagreement or fight,
Blinded by the need for another,
Instead of seeing another sleepless night,

It'll be right someday I'm hopeful as fuck,
The right one will come along,
I'm in a row just missing the duck,
Lined up walking the path,
I'll find it with all the luck!

17. You

Damn I miss kissing you,
God damn I'm missing you,
Damnit I'm wishing you,
Still needed me like I need you,
To stay happy with you,
To think its you,
The one who make me happy it's you,
Spending time with you,
Making memories with you,
Bringing smiles its true it's you,
Smiles and true blue you,
Over the moon with you,
Never untrue with you,
Genuine feelings for you,
Never enough time with you,
Always happy to see you,
Never regret spending time with you,
Because I love you

18. Life's mystery

Happy like I don't know,
Sad like shoveling wet snow,
Heavy as fuck,.
Ready to flow,
Ready to project my love,
Spew it out,
Bring some happiness,
Contentious doubt,
Just know I'll be here,
Stoked to be alive,
Knowing I'm exceeding expectations,
Knowing I'm beyond Drs expirations,
Too Ornery to die,
Fighters fight,
Too much pride to quit,
To much to drink a time or two,
So many memories,
Shared and legit,
Like pastures and hogs,
Over that bbq pit,

Radom lost orchards,
And a surprising treat at the olive pit,
To oceans full of fish,
Counting all those stars I wished,
Did it get me what I asked,
That wish was 15 years ago in the past,
Just know I'm here now,
In this reality that is,
Knowing where I started,
Where it began,
It lead me to this future,
Where I am.

19. See past

Can you see me,
Past the oxygen cord,
Past a physical disability,
You will find a kind word,
Some positivity,
A bright light ready to shine,
Ready for love to grow,
Grow so bright because you were blind,
In the fairest of ways,
Saw past my lack of oxygen,
Saw how far I could blaze,
How I can make you happy forever,
The rest of our days,
Instead of the rat race,
Chasing a bank account or a pretty face,
When all you need is tenderness,
And warm embrace,
A Love that is infinite,
A Love At a frantic pace,
A love that's strong,

So ornate and pretty like lace,
Full of flavor,
never short on taste,
Lovely morsels of love,
So full of kindness,
Thick like paste,
Tantalizingly amazing,
Perfectly spaced,
To win,
Race the race,
Face to face,
Love laced,
Confided in,
Covered and baste!
Did you see me?

20. Bull

Tied and twisted,
Full on torrents,
Flood then misted,
Bent down and listing,
Off center,
High revving piston,
Too many feelings lost,
Lop sided and cold,
Frigid frosted process,
Rusty and old,
Lost feelings let's toss them,
Bring back the numb and happy,
Too much to trim,
Cut off the excess,
Done lost it,
Run it through the wringer and squash it,
Just remember to jump in the mosh pit,
Sing with the choir,
Preach from the pulpit,
Remember the rest is all just bull spit!!

21. Alignment

The way I look at a magic moment,
Lost in precise alignment,
Do I opt out,
Or do the assignment,
Bring myself up to snuff,
Learn myself more,
Perfect consignment,
Be true to yourself,
Tougher than tough,
Let yourself,
Putt from the rough,
Don't be scared to learn or do more,
Keep trying to impress,
New awakenings to explore,
New faces to adore,
Doors shut but there's always a new door,
So much up side,
Grow ripped and torn,
New roads to travel,
Prick your finger,

Leave it to me to find the thorn,
I'm gonna spice up life,
New experiences are on the menu,
I'm tired of treading water,
And chewing life full of sinew,
Never breaking down,
Always ready to continue,
Giving everything within you,
To be valued like a higher prize,
Over the valley up the rise,
To the beautifully sunsetted sky,
That day will come in time,
The way I look at that magic moment,
Too lost and precise to align.